ARTIFICIAL INTELLIGENCE FOR SENIORS

HOW USING AI CAN IMPROVE YOUR LIFE

Peter Thorpe

Table of Contents

CHAPTER 1: INTRODUCTION

Hello, my name is Peter Thorpe and I'm about to turn 80 years of age. I've always been passionate about learning, and these days, I happily dedicate much of my time to exploring new skills and knowledge. My insatiable thirst for learning keeps my mind engaged and my brain active.

Lately, I've become captivated by Artificial Intelligence (AI). AI is transforming our lives, influencing how we work, play and interact with the world. From virtual assistants on smartphones, to chatbots and self-driving cars, AI is seamlessly integrating into our daily lives.

Unfortunately, a lot of mature aged people, who didn't grow up with computers and the internet, feel anxious about using technology and believe it's too late to learn about it. I understand that AI might seem complex and intimidating at first glance. However, here's the good news: *Accessing and using AI is not difficult at all, once you know how. And the benefits it can bring are truly life changing.*

This book aims to bridge that gap. It will show you how you can easily embrace AI to unlock new opportunities for learning, creativity, and fun.

So, come with me on an exhilarating journey into the captivating world of AI. Get ready for an adventure full of pleasant surprises and enjoyable activities that will make your learning experience both fun and exciting.

THINGS YOU CAN DO WITH AI

The limits of AI are virtually endless and expanding every day. Here are just some of the topics we will explore in this book:

1. Informational Questions: Ask about or check facts, definitions, explanations, or general knowledge on various topics. AI can provide information, explanations, and answers to a wide range of questions on various topics.

2. How-To Questions: Inquire about instructions or explanations on how to perform tasks or achieve a certain goal. AI can provide step-by-step instructions for tasks, recipes, DIY projects and more.

3. Opinions and Recommendations: Seek advice, recommendations, or opinions on various subjects. Get personalized recommendations for books and movies based on your personal likes and preferences.

4. Creative Prompts: Request assistance with creative writing, brainstorming ideas, or generating content, stories, poems or even jokes.

5. Problem-Solving & Brainstorming: If you're facing a challenge, describe the issue, and AI can help you brainstorm potential solutions.

6. Exploratory Questions: Discuss philosophical topics, futuristic scenarios, *"what if"* scenarios, and other thought-provoking subjects.

7. Educational Queries: Ask about concepts in science, history, mathematics and more, whether you're a student or simply curious.

8. Current Events: Inquire about recent news, developments or trends in various fields from around the globe.

9. Language and Communication: Seek assistance with grammar, language usage and communication advice. AI can also generate human-like text for articles, essays, stories, emails and more.

10. Write Speeches: From time to time, most of us are called on to make a speech. It might be at a milestone birthday party for you or a friend, daughter or grandson's 21st birthday or wedding. AI will write it for you in any style you wish. e.g. Serious, heart-felt or humorous, etc.

11. Emulating Characters: AI can simulate conversations in the style of famous personalities or fictional characters. e.g. Ask AI to write in the style of *Shakespeare* or *Hemingway*!

12. Summarization: AI can summarize long articles, documents, or passages of text. For instance, have you ever had to sign a long-winded legal document and found it very hard to understand? Simply copy and paste it into AI and ask it to summarize it in simple language!

13. Storytelling: AI can generate imaginative and engaging stories based on prompts. That could be a bedtime story for your grandkids or the outline of the world's next great novel.

14. Learn to Play Songs: AI can write song tabs for guitar or other instruments. It can even show you how to play chords and melodies using a bar chart of the strings and frets. It can even write original songs!

15: Travel Planning: Plan your next holiday using AI. Describe the type of destination, whether it's a beach getaway, African safari or exploring a certain city or country. Ask for recommendations on airline travel and hotels in your budget, etc.

16: Image Creation: AI image creators let you make images either just for fun or important tasks like greeting cards and invitations, etc. Just type in the image you want in text and AI will do the rest!

17: Health and Wellness Planning: Create tailor-made exercise plans with AI to promote your well-being and vitality. Seek dietary advice and get delicious recipes for a balanced and nutritious diet.

18: Financial and Wealth Management: AI can assist in creating and maintaining a budget, and help you manage your finances wisely. Get insights on potential investment opportunities and making smarter financial decisions. Plan your retirement with AI's expert guidance on savings, social security and pension options.

19. A Conversational Partner: AI can engage in interactive and dynamic conversations on a wide range of topics. It's just like having a full-time conversational partner to converse with.

20: Entertainment and Fun: Enjoy a good laugh with AI's collection of jokes and riddles. Engage in brain-stimulating games and puzzles for mental agility and entertainment. Ask for fun facts, trivia questions or information about your favorite hobbies, sports or interests.

SUMMARY
That's just a taste of what to expect. There's lots more! Embrace the possibilities AI offers and make it your trusted companion on this exciting journey. With the power of AI, we will unlock new avenues of learning, creativity, and fun to enrich your life and make the most of each day.

Using AI on a regular basis will help keep your mind active and enhance your life. Remember, age is just a number, and the world is at your fingertips!

Happy exploring!

CHAPTER 2: WHAT IS ARTIFICAL INTELLIGENCE?

Artificial Intelligence (AI) pertains to the creation of computer systems capable of carrying out tasks that usually demand human intelligence. These tasks include reasoning, learning, problem-solving, and decision-making and even learning from experience.

One of the early pioneers of AI was a man called Alan Turing. Turing was a British computer scientist and mathematician and is widely recognized as the father of AI. You may have heard his name before, he was credited as the main person who cracked the *German Enigma Code* that helped Britain win World War 2.

One of Turing's notable contributions to AI, is the concept of the *Turing Test*. In 1950, in his paper *"Computing Machinery and Intelligence,"* Turing proposed a test to determine a machine's ability to exhibit human-like intelligence. The Turing Test involves a human judge engaging in natural language conversations with both a human and a machine (which could be a computer program or an AI model). When the judge is unable to consistently differentiate between the machine's and the human's responses, the machine is considered to have successfully passed the test, demonstrating a degree of artificial intelligence.

Turing's work on the Turing Test and his ideas about machine intelligence, laid the foundation for the field of AI. He envisioned that a machine capable of holding intelligent conversations could be considered intelligent in its own right, leading to discussions about machine learning, natural language processing, and the quest to create machines that can mimic human thought processes.

While Turing's work was ground-breaking, it's important to note that the Turing Test is not without its critics and limitations. Some argue that passing the Turing Test does not necessarily indicate true human-like intelligence, as it primarily focuses on mimicking human behavior rather than deep understanding.

MACHINE LEARNING
Machine Learning is the backbone of AI. This is similar to the way our brains work. It enables machines to learn from data and experiences, improving their performance over time. Imagine teaching tricks to a dog. The more it practices these tricks, the better it becomes at performing them. Machine Learning works in a similar way. The program becomes smarter as it absorbs new information.

Data is the fuel that powers AI, with what is known as algorithms. An algorithm is a set of step-by-step instructions or rules, that a computer follows to solve a particular problem or achieve a specific task. Algorithms are the building blocks of most software and are used in a wide range of applications, from simple calculations to complex data analysis and artificial intelligence.

DIFFERENT TYPES OF AI
Not all AI systems are the same, there are many different types. Here is a brief description of the main types of AI available at present:

NARROW AI
Let's start with Narrow AI, also known as Weak AI. This type of AI is excellent at performing simple tasks really well. For example, think of the voice assistant on your smartphone, like *Siri* or *Alexa*. They can answer questions, set reminders, and perform simple tasks, but they are not capable of doing everything a human can do. Narrow AI is the most common type of AI we encounter in our daily lives.

REACTIVE MACHINES
Reactive Machines represent a basic form of AI that doesn't possess memory or the ability to learn from past experiences. Reactive Machines can only make decisions based on their existing data and rules. For example, a chess-playing machine that uses pre-programmed moves, without learning from the players, would come under this category.

GENERAL AI
General AI, also known as *Strong AI* or *Artificial General Intelligence* (AGI), is the dream of creating a machine that possesses human-like intelligence. Unlike Narrow AI, which is specialized in one area, General AI could understand, learn, and apply knowledge across multiple domains. However, at time of writing, we are still a long way away from achieving General AI, and it is still an area of ongoing research and development.

SELF-AWARE AI
Self-aware AI refers to an advanced form of artificial intelligence that not only possesses general intelligence but also exhibits self-awareness, consciousness, or a sense of identity.

In essence, self-aware AI would be aware of its own existence, thoughts, emotions, and experiences, in the same way humans are aware of their own consciousness. This would go beyond mere decision-making, based on data and patterns; the AI would have a subjective experience of its own existence. These machines would not only understand the world around them, but also have a sense of their existence, like the machine called *Hal,* in the movie *2001 a Space Odyssey*. The development of Self-aware AI is currently still in the realm of science fiction and raises significant ethical questions and possibly even potential threats to mankind.

PLEASE NOTE:
For the purposes of this book, we will be dealing mainly with Narrow AI and in particular a program called **ChatGPT**, which is based on this technology. You do not need to know any of the above in order to use and enjoy ChatGPT. These examples are simply to expand your knowledge of AI and give you an insight into where all this may be going.

CHAPTER 3: AN INTRODUCTION TO CHATGPT

You may have heard of an AI chatbot called **ChatGPT**?
ChatGPT is among the most widely used models for making
AI accessible to the general public. Before I introduce you to
ChatGPT, let me first make clear the difference between a
search engine like Google and an *AI chatbot* like ChatGPT.
The basic difference lies in their primary functions and how
they source information or interact with users.

A search engine like Google for instance, is designed
primarily for retrieving information from the vast amount of
data available on the internet. Users input keywords or
phrases related to what they're looking for, and the search
engine provides a list of relevant websites, documents,
images or videos that contain information that matches the
user's query. This often produces thousands of results. It's
then up to you to sort through the list and find what you are
looking for.

ChatGPT, on the other hand, is an AI equipped chatbot
designed for natural language processing and generation. It
simulates human-like conversations and interactions. Users
can input prompts or questions in natural language, and
ChatGPT generates responses in natural language, based on
patterns it has learned from its training data.

ChatGPT can be used for a variety of tasks, including
answering questions, providing explanations, generating text,
offering suggestions, and engaging in more interactive and
dynamic conversations. Unlike a search engine, which
retrieves existing content from the internet, ChatGPT
generates new content on the fly, based on the input it
receives.

OK so now we've made that clear, let's have a closer look at
ChatGPT.

GPT is an abbreviation for '*Generative Pre-trained Transformer*'. So, ChatGPT enables users to virtually chat with GPT. ChatGPT can understand and generate human-like text based on the input it receives. You can ask questions and receive answers in plain human language, just as you would with a real person. It's like a friendly virtual assistant that you can talk to, ask questions, brainstorm or have a conversation with.

ChatGPT was developed by a company called OpenAI. OpenAI was founded by Elon Musk and five other investors. It has also received funding from various sources, including venture capital firms and technology companies.

Microsoft became a partner with OpenAI in 2019, when they invested $1 billion to support the research and development of Artificial General Intelligence (AGI). They claim this partnership aims to advance AI technology and explore ways to harness AGI for the benefit of humanity.

With its conversational abilities, ChatGPT can be used for various applications. It has the ability to address queries, acknowledge errors, question inaccurate assumptions, and decline unsuitable demands. ChatGPT has since been integrated into various platforms and services to assist users in their day-to-day tasks and interactions.

ChatGPT uses a form of Narrow AI. That means it lacks the broad understanding and general intelligence that would be characteristic of a General AI. It relies on the patterns it has learned from a vast amount of data to generate responses, but it does not possess consciousness or awareness.

And, while it can generate impressive responses, it may sometimes produce incorrect or nonsensical answers. Moreover, it does not have a true understanding of context or the ability to comprehend, like humans do. In other words, it can't think like a human, although it sometimes gives the impression to users that it can! Additionally, it can be sensitive to the input phrasing, meaning slight changes in the way a question is posed, can yield totally different responses.*

Overall, ChatGPT represents a significant advancement in natural language processing and AI-driven text generation, but it is essential to use it responsibly and be mindful of its limitations to ensure the best user experience.

* **Footnote:** *One of the things you will learn from this book, is how to pose questions in the best way to get the right answer. This is very important to get the most out of using AI systems like ChatGPT.*

CHAPTER 4: THE HISTORY OF CHATGPT

The quest for creating computers that can understand and communicate with humans has a long history, dating back to the early 1950s. One of the earliest attempts at conversational AI was an early chatbot called ELIZA, developed in 1966 by Joseph Weizenbaum at the *Massachusetts Institute of Technology*. ELIZA used pattern matching to respond to user inputs and was a precursor to more sophisticated conversational AI systems.

In the following decades, advancements in machine learning and natural language processing led to the development of more capable language models. In 2015, computers emerged that were able to generate contextually relevant responses. The real breakthrough came in 2017 with the introduction of the "Transformer" architecture. Transformers, a type of deep learning model, revolutionized natural language processing and allowed computers to generate highly coherent and contextually accurate text.

In 2020, OpenAI made a significant impact with the release of GPT-3. GPT-3 demonstrated unparalleled language capabilities, including understanding context, answering complex questions, and generating creative text.

Building on the success of GPT-3, OpenAI launched ChatGPT in 2021. ChatGPT took conversational AI to new heights, enabling dynamic and interactive conversations. Users could now engage in chats, ask questions, seek advice, and receive friendly responses, making it feel just like interacting with a knowledgeable human being.

ChatGPT found its way into various applications, including customer support, content creation, language translation, and educational assistance. Its versatility and user-friendly interface made it accessible to a wide range of individuals and industries.

With the growing prevalence of conversational AI, ethical considerations and responsible AI practices came into prominence. OpenAI and other companies recognized the importance of addressing biases, misinformation, and misuse of AI technology. Transparency and responsible development became key pillars to ensure the positive impact of AI on society.

As we look to the future, the journey of ChatGPT is only the beginning of a long and exciting road for conversational AI. Ongoing research and advancements in technology, will likely lead to even more sophisticated and empathetic AI companions. The dream of creating AI that genuinely understands and interacts with humans, continues to inspire innovation, opening a world of possibilities for the future of AI.

CONCLUSION:
AI comes in various forms, each with its unique capabilities and limitations. The world of AI is changing rapidly and has the potential to improve our lives in many ways. At the same time, it's important to think about the ethics and dangers involved. Hopefully, we can use its strengths to create a better future.

CHAPTER 5: HOW DOES CHATGPT WORK?

In the previous chapter, we talked about the history of ChatGPT. Now, let's journey a little deeper and uncover how it was created and how it works.

ChatGPT was created by a collaborative effort from a bunch of brilliant scientists. Their aim was to teach a computer to understand human language and respond like a conversational partner. This behavior was learned from heaps of text that humans write, absorbing knowledge like a sponge, picking up the nuances and patterns of the spoken word.

It learned primarily from a massive amount of text data collected from the internet, including books, articles, websites, and other written content. Although the exact details of its creation are a closely guarded secret, it is said this included over 300,000 books. This diverse collection of text and data is what helps ChatGPT understand human language and generate responses that mimic natural conversation. This extensive training process allowed ChatGPT to acquire a wide range of knowledge and language patterns, enabling it to provide coherent and contextually relevant responses.

At its core, ChatGPT is like a gigantic collection of conversations, stories, and information. When you ask it a question or say something, it searches through this vast collection to find the best-fitting response, in a similar way to how a human recalls a story or fact to answer someone's question.

ChatGPT's way of talking is based on patterns it found in all the text it read. It doesn't truly understand like humans do, but it's fantastic at predicting what might come next in a conversation. So, it crafts responses that usually make sense, even though it's not thinking like a person.

At time of writing, the basic version ChatGPT3.5 may be used for free. *That's right – NO CHARGE!*

You may be thinking: "Why would a company spend more than a billion dollars to create a really smart machine like ChatGPT and then let millions of people use it at no cost?"

That's a good question and I thought the best person to answer this question was ChatGPT. This is its reply:

CHATGPT: The reasoning behind this seemingly generous move is rooted in several strategic considerations.

Firstly, by offering ChatGPT for free, the company can gather a massive user base. This extensive usage generates valuable data on how people interact with the technology and the types of questions they ask. This data becomes a treasure trove for refining and improving the AI model, making it smarter and more effective over time.

Secondly, providing free access builds goodwill and establishes the company's brand as a pioneer in democratizing AI. This positive image can lead to broader public recognition and trust, potentially resulting in more partnerships, collaborations, and business opportunities.

Thirdly, the company can develop premium or subscription-based services around ChatGPT. These advanced features can cater to businesses, professionals, or users who require specialized or higher-level interactions. This revenue stream can offset the initial investment and maintenance costs, allowing both free and premium users to coexist.

Lastly, the widespread use of ChatGPT contributes to its own improvement through a concept known as "training on more data." As millions of users engage with the system, it's exposed to a diverse array of inputs and requests. This exposure helps it understand and respond to a wide range of topics and contexts, enhancing its overall usefulness.

In summary, OpenAI's decision to invest in creating advanced AI models and offering them for free, aligns with their mission to ensure the benefits of AI are accessible to everyone, while also serving their strategic and research-driven goals. The balance between open access and potential monetization strategies, helps them achieve both their altruistic and practical objectives.

So, there you have it. As to how long you will be able to use it for free – *that's another question!*

ChatGPT3.5 is currently free to use for end-users. However, OpenAI is testing a paid version of its product which offers better access and improved results. Sam Altman, CEO of OpenAI, hinted there will be more upcoming paid versions in a tweet, noting, *"We will have to monetize it somehow at some point, the compute costs are eye-watering".*

This is understandable. At some point, investors will expect a return on their massive investment. Meanwhile, it's hoped that OpenAI will maintain a bare-bones free version of ChatGPT. This may mean in future, access to the free version could be restricted due to demand, and users potentially might have to wait in queues. They may even decide to include some form of advertising on the platform. I feel this would be a small sacrifice to make, given the extraordinary benefits of using it.

CHAPTER 6: GETTING STARTED WITH CHATGPT

Ok – I think it's about time to get you started on your journey – discovering and exploring AI and ChatGPT.

Here is a step-by-step guide to using ChatGPT.

1. Internet Connection: You will need an internet connection on your computer or device. ChatGPT operates online, so a reliable connection is essential.

2. Type of Device: You can use ChatGPT on a computer, tablet or smartphone. Choose the device that's most convenient for you.

3. Start an OpenAI Account: (Optional): You can access ChatGPT without opening an account by using plugins on your web browser, for instance. However, there is no charge for using the free version so you may as well open an account.

Simply go to the OpenAI website at https://openai.com/ on your computer and click on **SIGN UP**. *(Note: Details on how to connect using mobile devices is below).*

Fill in the necessary information, such as your name, email address, phone number and create a password. You don't need credit cards etc., for a free account. ChatGPT needs your phone number to verify you are a real person, but You can also sign in using your Google, Microsoft or Apple ID.

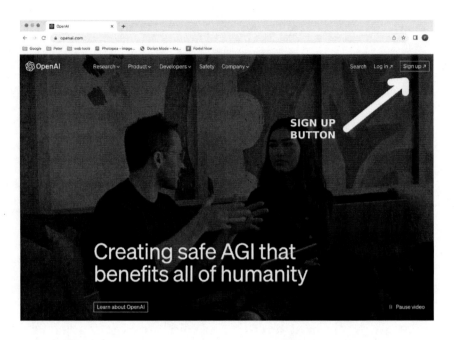

Go to OpenAI.com and click on the SIGN UP button.

Important: *Make a note of which ever method you use, because when you go to sign in again next time, you will need to sign in with the same authorization method.*

4. Accessing ChatGPT: Once you're logged in, navigate to the ChatGPT section of the website. This is where you'll interact with the AI.

5. Start a Session: You'll see a text box towards the bottom of the screen, where you can type your prompts or questions. Simply type in your message to start a conversation with ChatGPT.

5. Interact with ChatGPT: ChatGPT will respond based on your prompts. You can ask questions, seek explanations, or have a general conversation.

6. Experiment: Don't hesitate to experiment with different prompts or questions to see how ChatGPT responds. You can also try adjusting your instructions to get more accurate or detailed answers. We'll go into to detail of how to do this in later chapters of this book.

7. Explore Features: Depending on the platform you're using, there might be additional features or options to explore. These might include adjusting the AI's tone, style, or level of detail in responses.

USING CHATGPT ON YOUR SMART PHONE OR TABLET

The mobile app for ChatGPT is now available for IOS at the Apple app store and for Android phones at the Google Play store. At the time of writing, it is available in over 30 countries and OpenAI are adding new countries all the time. So, hopefully by the time you read this it will be available in your country.

To get started simply visit your app store and search for the ChatGPT app. Download the app and follow the simple instructions on your screen.

Once you have installed the app on your mobile device, it's very easy to use.

Note: If you are over the age of 15 and you can't type at 100 words per minute using two thumbs on your phone – don't worry! You can simply speak to ChatGPT, and it will convert your speech into text! Just tap the icon in the right-hand side of the text box and speak. When you have finished recording tap to stop recording and it will revert to text. *(See diagram below)*

When using ChatGPT on a mobile device you can use speech.

Note: Using speech input on a computer is possible too by invoking the voice recognition feature. Both **Windows PC** and **Mac computers** can use voice typing. You need to check your system's settings to set up speech recognition.

CHAPTER 7: TIPS FOR USING CHATGPT

ChatGPT will respond to your questions and prompts with human-like answers.

WHAT'S THE DIFFERENCE BETWEEN A QUESTION AND A PROMPT?

A question or a prompt are both forms of communication that initiate a response or interaction, but they have distinct characteristics and purposes:

QUESTIONS

A question, is a sentence or phrase used to elicit information, seek clarification, or engage in a dialogue. Questions are typically structured to prompt a specific type of response, such as an answer or an explanation. They are fundamental tools for communication and learning, enabling us to gather information, express curiosity, and deepen our understanding of a subject.

Example: *"Which animals always sleep standing up?"*

ChatGPT can also answer **contextual** questions. A contextual question is a type of question that considers the surrounding circumstances, details, or specific situation related to a topic. Instead of asking for general information or facts, a contextual question requires a deeper understanding of the subject matter and may involve specific conditions, background information or scenarios.

Contextual questions aim to gather insights or solutions that are tailored to a given context, making the response more relevant and useful. These questions often start with phrases like *"In the case of,"* *"Considering that,"* or *"Given the situation,"* and they help to address nuanced issues, individual preferences, or unique scenarios.

For instance, asking, *"What are some recommended travel destinations?"* is a general question. While asking *"What are some recommended travel destinations in Canada for a family with four young children?"* provides context that allows for more precise recommendations based on the family's needs and circumstances.

ChatGPT can also address **open-ended** questions. Here's a practical demonstration of an open-ended question. I asked ChatGPT the following:

Me: Complete this sentence please: I woke up this morning and the sun was shining so

CHATGPT: *I woke up this morning and the sun was shining so brightly, casting a warm glow across the room.*

Me: Continue on please

CHATGPT: *I woke up this morning and the sun was shining so brightly, casting a warm glow across the room. Its rays gently peeked through the curtains, illuminating everything in a soft, golden light. The promise of a beautiful day stretched before me, filling my heart with a sense of positivity and excitement.*

See how ChatGPT understands not just the question but the context of the sentence? So, if I change the context of the question ChatGPT will respond. Watch what happens:

ME: That's great thanks. Complete this sentence please and write a paragraph of text about it: *I woke up this morning and the sun was shining so I*

CHATGPT: *I woke up this morning and the sun was shining so **invitingly**, painting the sky with hues of warm gold and soft pink.*

As I rubbed the sleep from my eyes and stretched my limbs, I couldn't help but feel a surge of energy coursing through me. The sun's gentle rays streamed through my window, casting a cheerful glow upon everything they touched. The world outside seemed to come alive with renewed vitality, as if nature itself had awakened from a peaceful slumber. Etc., etc.

In that instance, it picked up the letter *"I"* at the end of the sentence and made it into a word, ***invitingly***, and continued from there. That's not what I wanted, so I responded:

Me: Let's try that again: I woke up this morning and the sun was shining so I (did something)

CHATGPT: *I woke up this morning and the sun was shining so invitingly that I couldn't resist taking a leisurely stroll through the park.*

The sunlight filtered through the leaves of the trees, creating playful patterns on the ground as I walked along the winding paths. The gentle warmth of the sun's embrace enveloped me, melting away the remnants of sleepiness and filling me with a sense of serenity. Birds serenaded from the branches above, their melodies harmonizing with the rustling of leaves in the breeze.

With each step, I felt a deeper connection to nature and a renewed appreciation for the simple pleasures of life. The vibrant colors of flowers in full bloom, the soothing sound of a nearby stream, and the distant laughter of children playing— all of it painted a scene of pure contentment.

As I continued my stroll, I couldn't help but smile at the beauty around me. The sun's presence was a gentle reminder that even in the midst of a busy world, there are moments of tranquility waiting to be savored. So, I walked on, absorbing the sunlight like a cherished gift and carrying its warmth with me throughout the day.

Me: Excellent thanks

CHATGPT: *You're welcome! If you have any more questions or need further assistance, feel free to ask. Have a wonderful day!*

PROMPTS

A prompt is a statement or instruction that serves as a starting point for generating a response. It can be open-ended or specific, and it often guides someone to continue or expand on a topic. Prompts are commonly used in creative writing, brainstorming, or when interacting with AI models like ChatGPT. In the context of using AI, a prompt sets the direction for the AI's generated text or output. How you word your prompts is very important to the quality of the answers you get. I'll cover this in more detail shortly.

In summary, while both prompts and questions initiate responses, a prompt often guides creative or generative tasks, and a question is specifically designed to elicit information, opinions, or insights. The choice between using a prompt or a question depends on the desired outcome and the nature of the interaction you wish to have.

Here's an example of a prompt:

Me: "Write a short story about how a man's dog helped solve a mysterious case".

CHATGPT: *In a quaint little town nestled between rolling hills, lived a man named Samuel. Samuel was known for his quiet demeanor and his steadfast companion, a loyal German Shepherd named Max. The town had always been peaceful, until a mysterious series of burglaries began to plague the community.*

27

One moonlit evening, as Samuel and Max were taking their customary stroll along the cobblestone streets, they stumbled upon a puzzling scene. The local bakery, usually bustling during the day, stood eerily silent with its windows shattered and pastries scattered. Samuel's curiosity was piqued, and he decided to investigate.

With Max at his side, Samuel began to piece together the clues left behind. Strange footprints, an overturned display case, and a peculiar pattern in the shattered glass – all of these details painted a confusing picture. Samuel's keen eye and Max's acute senses soon revealed that there was more to these burglaries than met the eye.

Over the next few weeks, as more incidents occurred, Samuel and Max tirelessly gathered information, connecting the dots between the various crime scenes. The townspeople grew increasingly worried, but Samuel's determination never wavered. Max, with his exceptional sense of smell, became an invaluable asset, tracking scents and leading Samuel to vital clues.

One fateful day, while sifting through old town records, Samuel stumbled upon a forgotten tale of a hidden treasure rumored to be buried beneath the town's square. As he delved deeper into the history, he realized that the burglaries were a diversion – a ploy to distract the townspeople from the real objective: finding the treasure.

With this newfound knowledge, Samuel and Max set out on their final investigation. Guided by Max's unwavering intuition, they followed a trail that led them to the heart of the town's square. Beneath a stone, they unearthed a chest filled with precious gems and artifacts that had been lost to time.

As news of their discovery spread, the townspeople were in awe of Samuel and Max's dedication and resourcefulness. The mystery that had gripped the town for so long had been solved, and it was all thanks to the unbreakable bond between a man and his dog. Samuel became a local hero, while Max's legendary reputation as a brilliant detective dog was cemented.

From that day forward, the town embraced its history and the treasure that lay beneath its cobblestones. Samuel and Max's story was a testament to the power of partnership, perseverance, and the unexpected heroes that can emerge from the most unlikely places. And as the sun set behind the rolling hills, Samuel and Max continued their walks, knowing that their unique adventures had forged an unbreakable connection between them and the town they loved.

That story would bring a tear to a glass eye! Seriously, you can see from that just how creative ChatGPT can be. Of course, sometimes it can be a little too verbose and flowery, but you can simply overcome this by asking it to rewrite it in a more straightforward manner by asking something like, *"Could you please simplify the story and make it more direct?"* ChatGPT will then rephrase the story using clear and concise language, focusing on presenting the facts and events without unnecessary embellishments.

VERY IMPORTANT

A prompt as the instruction you give to the AI before it generates its answer. Using the right prompt is crucial to getting the answer you are looking for. Your prompt needs to provide the necessary context and guidance to help the AI understand your intention and generate relevant responses. Using the right prompts will result in higher-quality and more accurate answers.

Here are some tips on how to improve your results by proving better prompts:

Tip 1: Be Clear and Specific

Poor Prompt: "Tell me about healthy eating."

Better Prompt: "I'm writing an article about promoting healthy eating habits among teenagers. Can you provide me with practical tips and ideas on how to make nutritious food appealing to this age group?"

Tip 2: State Your Objective

Poor Prompt: "What can you tell me about climate change?"

Better Prompt: "I'm preparing a presentation for my local Toastmasters Group on the consequences of climate change. Can you help me by providing key facts, real-life examples, and suggestions for engaging the audience?"

Tip 3: Use Contextual Details

Poor Prompt: "Explain how to grow flowers."

Better Prompt: "I'm starting a beginner's gardening guide and want to include a section on growing colorful flowers like roses and tulips. Can you walk me through the step-by-step process, including soil preparation, planting, and ongoing care?"

Tip 4: Ask Open-Ended Questions

Poor Prompt: "Is virtual reality used in education?"

Better Prompt: "I'm researching the impact of virtual reality on education. Can you provide me with examples of how VR is currently being integrated into classrooms to enhance learning experiences?"

Tip 5: Break Down Complex Questions

Poor Prompt: "How does quantum computing work?"

Better Prompt: "I'm trying to explain quantum computing in simple terms to my 16 year old son. Can you break down the basics, such as what qubits are and how they differ from traditional bits?"

Tip 6: Provide Examples

Poor Prompt: "Talk to me about renewable energy."

Better Prompt: "I'm writing a children's book that introduces the concept of renewable energy. Could you give me examples of solar and wind power that I can use to explain these ideas in a kid-friendly way?"

Tip 7: Use Multi-Turn Interactions

Poor Prompt: "What are the benefits of exercise?"

Better Prompt: "I'm interested in the long-term benefits of regular exercise. Can you provide me with a list of advantages that range from improved cardiovascular health to stress reduction?"

Tip 8: Specify Output Format

Poor Prompt: "Tell me about famous scientists."

Better Prompt: "I'm putting together a timeline of influential scientists throughout history. Could you provide me with brief summaries of five notable scientists along with their key discoveries?"

Tip 9: Set Constraints

Poor Prompt: "Explain how nuclear reactors work."

Better Prompt: "I'm looking for a simple explanation of nuclear reactors suitable for a high school physics class. Please use clear language and avoid technical jargon."

Tip 10: Use Suggested User Profile

Poor Prompt: "Give me some information about AI."

Better Prompt: "I'm trying to get a better understanding of AI and I'm curious about its real-world applications. Can you provide me with examples of how AI is used in healthcare, finance, and entertainment?"

Using these examples, you can see how adding context, specifying your purpose, and tailoring your prompts to your specific needs, can lead to more precise and useful responses from ChatGPT.

THE "ACT AS" PROMPT

Another great tip to writing good prompts is to use the **"Act as"** prompt. The *"Act as"* prompt instructs ChatGPT to generate responses as if it were assuming a specific role. This allows it to generate answers tailored to that role's expertise or perspectives.

Here are a few examples of how it can work effectively:

Prompt: "Act as an AI expert and explain the concept of machine learning to someone with no technical background."

Response: "Machine learning is like teaching computers to learn from examples. Imagine training a dog: you show it pictures of different animals, and it learns to recognize them. Similarly, computers use data to learn patterns and make predictions."

Prompt: "Act as a travel advisor and recommend the best destinations for a family vacation."

Response: "For a family vacation, consider destinations like Orlando for its theme parks, Yellowstone National Park for outdoor adventures, or a beach resort like Miami for relaxation and water activities."

Prompt: "Act as a history teacher and explain the significance of the Industrial Revolution in simple terms."

Response: "The Industrial Revolution was a time when machines changed how things were made. It led to factories, which made goods faster. This transformed how people lived and worked."

Prompt: "Act as a health expert and give advice on maintaining a healthy lifestyle."

Response: "To stay healthy, eat balanced meals with fruits, veggies, and whole grains. Exercise regularly, get enough sleep, and manage stress through activities like yoga or meditation."

Prompt: "Act as a sci-fi author and come up with a short story idea involving time travel."

Response: "In a future world, scientists discover a way to send messages back in time. A young historian receives a mysterious message from the past, leading to a thrilling quest to change history."

Using the *"Act as"* prompt is a great way for you to immerse yourself in different roles and scenarios, enabling you to generate content that aligns with the context you've provided.

CHAPTER 8: FEEDBACK AND TRAINING CHATGPT

At this point, you may be wondering why I would bother talking to ChatGPT like I would talk to a human being? After all, it's just a machine and as it doesn't have feelings. Why would I bother being polite and say please and thank you, etc.?

There's a reason for this and it's not just because my mother brought me up to always be polite! Feedback is vitally important to ChatGPT. Positive feedback helps reinforce accurate and helpful responses, while negative feedback helps the system learn and avoid repeating mistakes.

There are several ways to provide feedback. Here is the simplest one:
When you use ChatGPT you will notice next to your response there are three small icons: a clipboard and two thumbs, one up and one down. It looks like this:

Here's what they represent and how you can use them:

1. **CLIPBOARD ICON:** The clipboard icon on the left, simply allows you to copy the text of the response to your clipboard. This is useful if you want to paste the response somewhere else, like in a document, email, or any other application.

2. **THUMBS UP ICON:** The thumbs up icon is used to indicate that you found the response helpful and accurate. If the response provided the information, you were looking for or answered your question satisfactorily, you can click the thumbs up icon to provide positive feedback.

3. **THUMBS DOWN ICON:** The thumbs down icon is used when you feel that the response was not helpful, accurate, or appropriate. If the response contained errors, misinformation or was not relevant to your query, you can click the thumbs down icon to provide feedback that the response needs improvement.

Using these icons helps improve performance over time by letting the system learn from user feedback. Positive feedback helps reinforce accurate and helpful responses, while negative feedback helps the system learn and avoid repeating mistakes.

When using the feedback icons, remember to use them thoughtfully and genuinely, based on the quality of the response. This helps in refining and enhancing the system's capabilities to better assist users in the future.

So, is it best to just use these icons or provide comments?

The answer is: both can be helpful for improving performance. The choice depends on what you're comfortable with and the complexity of your feedback. Using the icons is a quick way of indicating the quality of a response. However, elaborating with comments can give the system more context and insights into how the responses are perceived. It's particularly helpful for cases where the response is more complex, and your feedback might be nuanced.

In short, both icons and comments have their place. Icons are convenient for quick feedback, while comments are valuable for offering more detailed thoughts. For instance, you might make the following comment: *"That's good but give me more detail".* Or *"Give it to me in simpler terms,"* etc. This type of feedback helps to "train" the system to the sort of answers you are looking for. Feel free to use the approach that best suits the situation and what you feel comfortable with.

CUSTOMISING CHATGPT

To customize ChatGPT, you provide a "prompt" that includes a few examples of how you want it to respond. You can even instruct it explicitly, like *"Answer in a cheerful tone"* or *"Explain like I'm talking to a child."* The more you interact with the customized prompts, the better ChatGPT becomes at understanding and matching your preferences.

Here are a few examples to help you understand how customization works in ChatGPT:

TONE AND STYLE: Let's say you're a cheerful person who likes using positive and friendly language. You can customize ChatGPT to respond in a similar upbeat tone. For instance, if you ask about the weather, instead of a plain response, ChatGPT might say, "The sun is shining and it's a wonderful day outside!"

SPECIFIC TOPICS: Let's say you are creating a website about gardening and wish to have a gardening expert, you can tailor it to comprehend gardening concepts and describe them in an easy-to-understand manner. This approach ensures that when you inquire about gardening techniques, ChatGPT can offer explanations that match the tone of your website.

PERSONAL PREFERENCES: Let's say you're a vegetarian and want cooking tips. You can customize ChatGPT to know your dietary preference. When you ask for recipes, it will provide vegetarian options instead of suggesting meat-based dishes.

PHRASING AND VOCABULARY: If you have a unique way of speaking or prefer certain words, you can teach ChatGPT your preferred phrasing. For example, if you often use informal language, ChatGPT can mimic that style in its responses.

ROLE PLAY OR STORYTELLING: If you're into creative writing or role-playing, you can customize ChatGPT to understand characters, settings, and storylines you're working on. It can then generate dialogues and descriptions that fit your fictional world.

SETTING CUSTOM INSTRUCTIONS

Now ChatGPT can be customized permanently to suit your needs. Custom instructions allow you to add preferences or requirements you'd like ChatGPT to consider when generating its responses.

Once you have set these, ChatGPT will consider your custom instructions for every conversation going forward. So, you won't have to repeat your preferences or information in every conversation.

For example, a teacher crafting a lesson plan, no longer must repeat that they're teaching 3rd grade science. Grocery shopping for a big family becomes easier, with the model accounting for 6 servings in the grocery list.

Customization will make ChatGPT understand and talk more like you want it to. These settings can be changed at any time to suit your needs.

HOW TO SET IT UP

When you login to ChatGPT, towards the bottom of the left-hand side of the page you will see three dots. This is a menu. If you click on the menu, you will see an option pop-up called **Custom Instructions**.

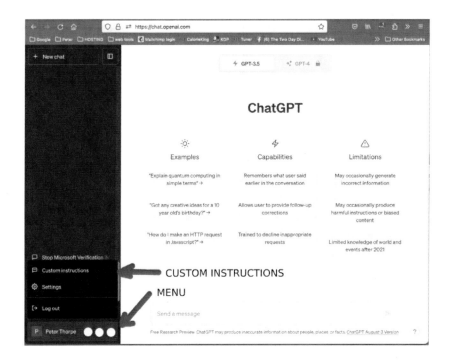

The menu and Custom Instructions buttons on ChatGPT.

When you click on *Custom Instructions* it will ask you questions about how you want to personalize your preferences. For instance, it will ask:

What would you like ChatGPT to know about you to provide better responses?

It then gives you some **thought starters** like this:

Where are you based?
What are your hobbies and interests?
What are some goals you have? Etc.

It also asks: *How would you like ChatGPT to respond?*

Long or short answers?
Formal or informal?
Should ChatGPT have opinions on topics or remain neutral?

Remember, while customization is powerful, it's based on patterns in the examples you provide. It might not always perfectly replicate your style, but it can certainly get close!

CHAPTER 9: PRACTICAL USES OF AI WITH EXAMPLES

You can ask ChatGPT a wide range of questions or prompts. Here are some examples of things you can ask:

INFORMATIONAL QUESTIONS:
Ask about or check facts, definitions, explanations, or general. AI can provide information, explanations, and answers to a wide range of questions on various topics.

EXAMPLE:

ME: What was the main event that triggered World War 2?

CHATGPT: *The main event that triggered World War 2 was the invasion of Poland by Germany on September 1, 1939. This invasion marked the beginning of a series of military actions and conflicts that quickly escalated into a global conflict involving many nations. The invasion of Poland prompted the United Kingdom and France to declare war on Germany on September 3, 1939, leading to the outbreak of World War 2.*

The invasion of Poland violated international agreements and treaties, and it demonstrated the aggressive expansionist policies of Nazi Germany under Adolf Hitler. This act of aggression set off a chain reaction of military alliances and conflicts that eventually engulfed much of the world in war, leading to six years of devastating conflict and significant geopolitical and societal changes.

HOW-TO QUESTIONS:
Inquire about instructions or explanations on how to perform a task or achieve a certain goal. AI can provide step-by-step instructions for tasks, recipes, DIY projects and more.

ME: Can you please tell me how to care for indoor plants?

CHATGPT: *Caring for indoor plants involves a few key steps to ensure they thrive. Here's a concise guide:*

1. Light: Place plants in appropriate light conditions – low, medium, or bright. Research your plant's needs.

2. Watering: Water when the top inch of soil is dry, but don't let plants sit in water. Avoid overwatering.

3. Humidity: Some plants like higher humidity. Mist leaves or use a humidity tray if needed.

4. Temperature: Keep plants away from extreme temperature fluctuations, drafts, and heating/cooling sources.

5. Pruning: Trim dead or yellowing leaves to promote growth. Pinch back tips for bushier growth.

6. Fertilizing: Feed with a balanced liquid fertilizer during the growing season (spring and summer).

7. Repotting: Repot when roots outgrow the pot. Choose a slightly larger container with drainage holes.

8. Pests: Regularly inspect for pests like mealybugs or spider mites. Treat promptly if detected.

9. Dusting and Cleaning: Keep leaves clean by wiping gently with a damp cloth to allow proper light absorption.

10. Research: Learn about your specific plants' needs. Each variety can have unique care requirements.

Remember, each plant type has specific needs, so adapt these steps accordingly. Observing your plants and responding to their conditions will help them thrive indoors.

OPINIONS AND RECOMMENDATIONS:
Seek advice, recommendations, or opinions on various subjects. Get personalized recommendations for books and movies based on your personal likes and preferences.

ME: Can you please recommend a book or books about people who have turned their lives around.

CHATGPT: *Absolutely, here are a few recommended books that highlight inspiring stories of individuals who have turned their lives around:*

"Can't Hurt Me: Master Your Mind and Defy the Odds" by David Goggins:
This book chronicles the incredible journey of David Goggins, who overcame significant challenges, including childhood trauma and obesity, to become a Navy SEAL, ultra-endurance athlete, and motivational speaker. His story is a testament to the power of determination and self-discipline.

"Unbroken: A World War II Story of Survival, Resilience, and Redemption" by Laura Hillenbrand: This gripping true story follows Louis Zamperini, an Olympic athlete turned WWII prisoner of war. It portrays his remarkable resilience, survival against the odds, and eventual redemption as he triumphs over adversity.

"Wild: From Lost to Found on the Pacific Crest Trail" by Cheryl Strayed: This memoir documents Cheryl Strayed's solo journey on the Pacific Crest Trail as she navigates grief, personal turmoil, and self-discovery. Her story showcases the transformative power of nature and resilience in the face of life's challenges.

4. "The Glass Castle" by Jeannette Walls: Jeannette Walls recounts her upbringing in a dysfunctional and poverty-stricken family. Despite the hardships, she eventually breaks free and builds a successful life. The book is a testament to the strength of the human spirit and the ability to overcome adversity.

These books offer powerful insights into the capacity for change, growth, and transformation in the face of adversity. They can serve as a source of inspiration and motivation for anyone seeking to turn their own life around.

CREATIVE PROMPTS:
Request assistance with creative writing, brainstorming ideas, or generating content, stories, poems or even jokes.

ME: Please write a short poem for me about a group of seniors who get together for coffee once a week to discuss the problems of the world.

CHATGPT:

In cozy cafes, their chairs entwine,
A circle of wisdom, hearts align,
Seniors, weathered by time's embrace,
Gather to share life's diverse grace.

With cups of warmth, they convene anew,
Stories and laughter, a vibrant hue,
Discussing the world's intricate seams,
Dreams and hopes, like soft moonbeams.

Problems of the world, they contemplate,
A tapestry woven with thoughts innate,
Through wrinkled hands and sparkling eyes,
They seek solutions that gently rise.

With empathy's touch, they understand,
Uniting their hearts, a caring hand,
In coffee's aroma, and tales unfurled,
They find solace and hope in this world.

A group of seniors, souls aglow,
With every sip, compassion flows,
In unity, they find their way,
Sipping hope together, come what may.

EMULATE CHARACTERS:

AI can simulate conversations in the style of famous personalities or fictional characters. e.g. Ask AI to write in the style of *Shakespeare* or *Hemingway*! For example:

ME: Excellent thanks. Now rewrite that in the style of Shakespeare please.

CHATGPT:

In yonder coffee nook, aged seats entwine,
A fellowship of elders, a weekly assign.
Their hearts, as one, united in accord,
As they sup on coffee, discourse is their word.

Wrinkles and lines, etchings of the years,
Stories of yore, and laughter that cheers.
Around the table, they gather and share,
Tales of life's journey, with wisdom to spare.

As cups clink and steam wafts to the skies,
Global conundrums within their eyes.
With nods and murmurs, they engage profound,
Discussing worldly trials that do confound.

'Tis not mere coffee, but unity's tether,
A refuge to face challenges together.
In the warmth of their circle, problems unfurled,
They find strength and solace in this world.

PROBLEM-SOLVING & BRAINSTORMING:
If you're facing a challenge, describe the issue, and
CHATGPT will help you brainstorm potential solutions.

ME: How can I get my grandchildren to stop spending so
much time on their smart phones?

CHATGPT: *To steer your grandchildren away from excessive
smartphone use, consider these strategies:*

*1. Set an Example: Show them a balanced approach by
limiting your own screen time and engaging in offline
activities.*

*2. Open Conversation: Have an open and honest discussion
about the effects of excessive screen time on health,
relationships, and productivity.*

*3. Establish Tech-Free Times: Designate specific times, like
during meals or before bedtime, as tech-free zones to
encourage face-to-face interactions.*

*4. Engage in Activities: Plan enjoyable activities they can
partake in, like outdoor games, crafts, or cooking, to divert
their attention from screens.*

*5. Discover New Interests: Help them explore hobbies or
interests that don't involve screens, fostering their creativity
and passions.*

*6. Family Bonding: Organize regular family activities, such as
board games or outings, to create lasting memories and
strengthen relationships.*

*7. Educate about Balance: Teach them about the importance
of balancing online and offline activities for a healthier
lifestyle.*

8. *Encourage Reading: Introduce them to books or audiobooks that pique their curiosity and ignite a love of reading.*

9. *Involve Friends: Encourage them to engage in social activities with friends where smartphones take a backseat.*

10. *Positive Reinforcement: Acknowledge and reward their efforts to reduce screen time with praise or small incentives.*

Remember, the goal is to foster a healthy relationship with technology while promoting other meaningful activities that contribute to their personal growth and well-being.

EXPLORATORY QUESTIONS:
Discuss philosophical topics, futuristic scenarios, *"what if"* scenarios, and other thought-provoking subjects.

ME: What if animals could communicate with humans in a language we understand? How might this affect our relationship with animals?

CHATGPT: *If animals could communicate with humans in a language we understand, it would undoubtedly revolutionize our relationship with the animal kingdom. Here's how things might change:*

1. **Deeper Understanding:** *We would gain insights into animals' thoughts, emotions, and needs. This understanding could lead to more compassionate treatment, as we'd be better equipped to address their well-being.*

2. **Environmental Awareness:** *Animals could share information about their habitats, migration patterns, and ecological concerns. This could lead to better conservation efforts and a heightened awareness of our impact on the environment.*

3. Ethical Considerations: *Clear communication might prompt us to rethink the ethics of animal farming, experimentation, and entertainment. We'd be confronted with the moral implications of our actions.*

4. Collaboration: *Animals could contribute unique insights to fields like agriculture and medicine. For example, they could help us understand natural remedies and sustainable farming practices.*

5. Interspecies Partnerships: *Working animals like service dogs or therapy animals could provide more direct input, improving their roles and enhancing the assistance they offer.*

6. Cultural Exchange: *The exchange of knowledge could lead to the development of rich cultural exchanges between humans and animals, fostering greater respect for their unique ways of life.*

7. Animal Rights: *With animals expressing their preferences, the concept of animal rights might evolve. They could participate in decisions affecting their lives, such as habitat protection or relocation efforts.*

8. Emotional Connection: *Communication could strengthen emotional bonds between humans and animals, as we understand their individual personalities and experiences.*

9. Conflict Resolution: *Misunderstandings between humans and animals, like wildlife encroachments in urban areas, could be addressed through dialogue and negotiation.*

10. Responsibility and Stewardship: *The responsibility of caring for animals could become even more pronounced, as we hear directly about their needs and experiences.*

While this "what if" scenario raises exciting possibilities, it would also present challenges, such as language barriers between species and the potential for exploitation. Yet, overall, it would likely lead to a more harmonious and empathetic coexistence between humans and the animal kingdom.

EDUCATIONAL QUERIES:
Ask about concepts in science, history, mathematics, and more, whether you're a student or simply curious.

ME: Please explain in very simple terms Einstein's theory of relativity in no more than 125 words.

CHATGPT: Of course! Einstein's theory of relativity is a ground-breaking idea about how time, space, and gravity work. There are two parts: Special Relativity and General Relativity.

Special Relativity says that time and space aren't absolute, but change depending on how fast you're moving. It introduced the famous equation $E=mc^2$, showing the connection between energy and mass.

General Relativity goes further, saying that gravity isn't just a force, but actually a bending of space and time around massive objects. This explains why planets orbit the Sun and how light gets bent around stars.

In a nutshell, Einstein's theory changed our understanding of the universe by linking together space, time, and gravity in a new way.

CURRENT EVENTS:
Inquire about news, developments or trends in various fields from around the globe.

ME: If both polar ice caps melted how much would the sea rise by?

CHATGPT: If both polar ice caps, including the Antarctic and Greenland ice sheets, were to melt completely, it is estimated that global sea levels could rise by about 216 feet (65.8 meters). This is a worst-case scenario and would have catastrophic effects on coastlines, ecosystems, and communities around the world.

However, it's important to note that the complete melting of both ice caps is a complex and unlikely scenario. The rate at which ice melts depends on various factors, including temperature, ocean currents, and feedback mechanisms. While the melting of polar ice caps is a concern due to ongoing climate change, the actual sea-level rise would depend on many variables and could unfold over an extended period of time.

Efforts to mitigate climate change, reduce greenhouse gas emissions, and take steps to protect vulnerable coastlines are crucial to prevent the most extreme sea-level rise scenarios from occurring.

LANGUAGE AND COMMUNICATION:
Seek assistance with grammar, language usage and communication advice. AI can also generate human-like text for articles, essays, stories, emails and more.

ME: Please write a short (less than 100 word) very humorous email inviting people to John's 60th Birthday party.

CHATGPT:

Subject: Turning Sixty and Still Rocking!

Hey there party animals,

You better believe it! Our dear friend John is hitting the big 6 0h, and it's time to celebrate like it's 1950... well, kinda.

Date: [Date]
Time: [Time]
Venue: [Venue]

Come join us for a night of vintage vibes, timeless tunes, and some seriously good cake. Don't worry, the candles won't set off the fire alarm – we promise!

So, grab your party hats, bring your finest wrinkles (John insists wrinkles are a badge of wisdom), and let's show him that 60 is the new 30... with a few bonus years of experience.

RSVP by [RSVP Date], and let's give John a night to remember (or at least a night he won't forget due to his memory pills)!

See you there, and don't forget to bring your best '60s dance moves!

Cheers,
[Your Name]

WRITE SPEECHES:
From time to time, most of us are called on to make a speech. It might be at a milestone birthday party for you or a friend, daughter or grandson's 21st birthday or wedding. ChatGPT will write it for you in any style you wish. e.g. Serious or humorous, etc.

ME: Please write a short (less than 100 word) speech for my daughter's wedding using humor. She and her husband to be, are very keen horse riders.

CHATGPT: *Ladies and gentlemen,*

Today, we gather to celebrate a love story that's as wild and wonderful as a gallop through an open field. As [Daughter's Name] and [Spouse's Name] embark on this journey, I can't help but notice the similarities between their love and their passion for horse riding.

Just like a perfect equestrian partnership, they've found balance, trust, and the ability to steer through life's obstacles together. And let's not forget, much like riding a spirited horse, marriage requires patience, a good sense of humor, and occasionally a helmet.

So, as we raise our glasses to this remarkable couple, let's toast to a love that's as strong as the bond between a rider and their faithful steed. May their journey be filled with joy, adventure, and plenty of stable ground.

Cheers to [Daughter's Name] and [Spouse's Name] – a love story that's a true gallop towards happiness!

SUMMARIZATION:
ChatGPT can summarize long articles, documents, or passages of text. For instance, have you ever had to sign a long-winded legal document and found it very hard to understand? Simply copy and paste it into ChatGPT and ask it to summarize it in simple language!

ME: Please simplify the following statement:

These provisions may be supplemented by, or replaced with, optional provisions connected with certain features that may be included by this arrangement, including where the arrangement involves a funding model which will require that the Government takes security, or commercially agreed terms for bonds which provide for security to be given, over particular assets, for which certain "Secured Transaction" provisions may need to be included.

CHATGPT: *Extra rules can be added or changed with other rules that relate to specific things included in this arrangement. This could be when the arrangement has a* *money plan needing the Government to make things safe, or when bonds have terms for safety over certain things. These special rules might be needed for some parts.*

STORYTELLING:
AI can generate imaginative and engaging stories based on prompts. That could be a bedtime story for your grandkids or the outline for the world's next great novel!

ME: Please give me an outline for a short story about a woman who travels to Argentina in the early 1800s hoping to meet the man of her dreams.

CHATGPT:

Title: Echoes of Tango Dreams

Chapter 1: A Daring Departure
Introduce the protagonist, yearning for adventure and romance.
Set in the early 1800s as she embarks on a journey to Argentina.
Express her fascination with the Argentine culture, especially the tango.

Chapter 2: The Enchanted City
Portray her arrival in Buenos Aires, captivated by its vibrant energy.
Describe her exploration of the city's streets and markets.

Chapter 3: Tango Dreams Unveiled
Introduce a mysterious tango dancer she's been hearing about.
Depict her attempts to meet him, leading to humorous situations.
Hint at the presence of another man, a local musician.

Chapter 4: Dance of Fate

Reveal her discovery that the tango dancer isn't who she thought.
Show her forming an unexpected connection with the musician.
Illustrate their shared dreams and conversations.

Chapter 5: Whispers of Love
Develop their relationship through shared experiences.
Describe a mesmerizing tango performance that deepens their bond.

Chapter 6: Echoes in Time
Convey their realization that their lives are diverging.
Depict their bittersweet farewell, leaving her with cherished memories.
End with her back home, dancing a tango-inspired dance, carrying the echoes of her Argentine journey.

Through these six chapters, the story captures the essence of the protagonist's adventure in Argentina, her unexpected encounters, and the transformative power of unexpected connections.

Warning: Before you write the next number 1 best-selling novel, make sure ChatGPT didn't just copy this from someone else's story. See the chapter later in this book about *PLAGIARISM & ETHICAL CONSIDERATIONS.*

LEARN TO PLAY SONGS:
ChatGPT can write song tabs for guitar or other instruments. It can show you chords and even show you how to play melodies using a bar chart of the strings and frets.

ME: Please create a words and chords for the song "Old Man River".

CHATGPT: *This classic song comes from the musical "Show Boat" and has been performed by various artists over the years. The song is typically played in the key of G, and the chords for the verses and chorus follow a simple pattern. Here's a basic chord progression along with the lyrics:*

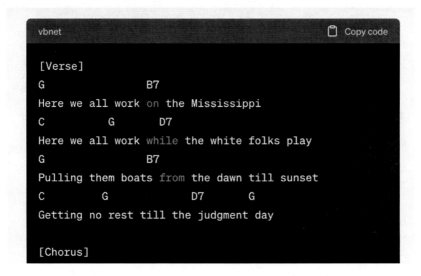

```vbnet
[Verse]
G                       B7
Here we all work on the Mississippi
C         G         D7
Here we all work while the white folks play
G                       B7
Pulling them boats from the dawn till sunset
C         G               D7       G
Getting no rest till the judgment day

[Chorus]
```

ME: Please show me the fingering for the C chord on guitar.

CHATGPT: *Of course, I'd be happy to help you with the C chord on the guitar! The C chord is one of the fundamental open chords and is commonly used in many songs. Here's how to play it:*

1. Place your ring (3rd) finger on the 3rd fret of the 5th string (A string).
2. Keep your middle (2nd) finger on the 2nd fret of the 4th string (D string).
3. Leave the 1st, 2nd, and 6th strings open (unfretted).
4. Mute the 3rd string (G string) by lightly touching it with the fleshy part of your middle finger.

The fingering positions should look like this:

```lua
e|---0---
B|---1---
G|---0---
D|---2---
A|---3---
E|---x---
```

Strum the C chord starting from the 5th string (A string) down to the high E string (the 1st string). Ensure that the strings you're not pressing down on (1st, 2nd, and 6th) remain open and can resonate freely.

Practice transitioning between the C chord and other chords to improve your chord changes. With practice, you'll be able to play the C chord smoothly and effortlessly. If you have any more questions or need further assistance, feel free to ask!

Question: Can ChatGPT create original music and lyrics?

ChatGPT can aid in generating original songs or music, but the extent to which it can do so effectively depends on factors like input, instructions, and human involvement in the creative process. It's best used as a tool to help spark ideas and provide inspiration, with the understanding that the final product might require human creativity and expertise to truly shine.

Also, if you're considering using AI-generated music for commercial purposes, make sure to understand any legal and ethical considerations regarding copyright and ownership of the generated content.

TRAVEL PLANNING:

Plan your next holiday using ChatGPT. Describe the type of destination, whether it's a beach getaway, African safari or exploring a certain city or country. Ask for recommendations on airline travel and hotels in your budget, etc.

ME: I'm planning a tour of the Bahamas. What advice would you give me and what recommendations have you got for places to visit?

CHATGPT: Planning a tour of the Bahamas is exciting! Here's some advice and recommended places to make your trip memorable:

Advice:

1. Research: Familiarize yourself with the Bahamas' islands, culture, and travel requirements, including visas and COVID-19 protocols.

2. Travel Season: The peak tourist season is December to April, but it's also pricier. Consider shoulder seasons (May-June, September-October) for better deals and fewer crowds.

3. Island Hopping: The Bahamas consists of 700 islands and cays. Consider hopping between a few to experience diverse landscapes and local flavors.

4. Water Activities: Snorkeling, scuba diving, and swimming with pigs at Exuma are must-do water activities.

5. Local Cuisine: Try conch dishes, Bahamian fish fry, and fresh seafood at local joints.

6. Cultural Etiquette: Respect local customs, including dressing modestly when not at the beach.

7. Health and Safety: *Stay hydrated, wear sunscreen, and keep an eye on weather updates during hurricane season (June-November).*

Recommended Places:

1. Nassau: *The capital city offers historical sites like Fort Fincastle, vibrant markets, and the stunning Cable Beach.*

2. Paradise Island: *Home to Atlantis Resort with water parks, casinos, and beautiful beaches.*

3. Exuma: *Swim with pigs at Pig Beach, explore the Exuma Cays Land and Sea Park, and enjoy pristine beaches.*

4. Abaco Islands: *Known for sailing, boating, and charming settlements like Hope Town.*

5. Andros: *Explore its blue holes, underwater caves, and the third-largest barrier reef.*

6. Grand Bahama Island: *Visit Freeport's Port Lucaya Marketplace and explore Lucayan National Park's underwater cave system.*

7. Bimini: *Famous for its clear waters, fishing, and Ernest Hemingway's connections.*

8. Eleuthera and Harbor Island: *Pink sand beaches, Glass Window Bridge, and historic Dunmore Town.*

9. Long Island: *Experience diving, Dean's Blue Hole (world's deepest blue hole), and local culture.*

10. Cat Island: *Relax on secluded beaches, explore historical sites, and learn about Bahamian folklore.*

Remember, each island has its unique charm, so choose based on your interests. Whether you're into water sports, cultural experiences, or simply relaxing on the beach, the Bahamas offers something for everyone.

Editor's tip:
There is a wealth of information available about travel on ChatGPT. Think of it as your very own personal travel consultant.

You can plan everything from exciting itineraries to practical travel tips, all tailored to your own preferences and interests. ChatGPT's extensive knowledge and AI-powered insights will elevate your travel planning experience to a whole new level. Whether you're seeking hidden gems in bustling cities or serene getaways off the beaten track, let ChatGPT be your trusted companion in crafting unforgettable journeys.

HEALTH AND WELLNESS PLANNING
Create tailor-made exercise plans with AI to promote your well-being and vitality. Seek dietary advice and get delicious recipes for a balanced and nutritious diet.

ME: Please give me a recipe for breakfast that contains less than 200 calories.

CHATGPT: *Certainly! Here's a simple and nutritious recipe for a low-calorie breakfast option:*

Scrambled Egg and Veggie Breakfast Bowl

Ingredients:

2 large eggs
1/2 cup diced bell peppers (any color)
1/4 cup diced tomatoes.
1/4 cup chopped spinach or kale.
Salt and pepper to taste.
Cooking spray or a small amount of olive oil for cooking

Instructions:

1. Heat a non-stick skillet over medium heat and lightly coat it with cooking spray or a small amount of olive oil.

2. Add the diced bell peppers and sauté for about 2-3 minutes until they start to soften.

3. Add the diced tomatoes and chopped spinach or kale to the skillet. Sauté for an additional 1-2 minutes until the vegetables are slightly cooked.

4. In a small bowl, whisk the eggs together with a pinch of salt and pepper.

5. Push the sautéed vegetables to one side of the skillet and pour the beaten eggs into the empty space.

6. Allow the eggs to cook undisturbed for a few seconds, then gently scramble them using a spatula.

7. Once the eggs are cooked to your desired consistency, combine them with the sautéed vegetables in the skillet.

8. Mix everything together and continue cooking for another minute to ensure the eggs are fully cooked and the vegetables are heated through.

9. Season with additional salt and pepper if needed.

10. Transfer the scrambled egg and veggie mixture to a serving bowl.

Enjoy your delicious and low-calorie scrambled egg and veggie breakfast bowl, packed with nutrients and under 200 calories! Feel free to customize the veggies and spices to your taste preferences.

FINANCIAL AND WEALTH MANAGEMENT

AI can assist in creating and maintaining a budget, and help you manage your finances wisely. Get insights on potential investment opportunities and help making smarter financial decisions. Plan your retirement with AI's expert guidance on savings, social security, and pension options.

I asked ChatGPT to give me an example:

ME: Please act as a financial advisor and give me an example of how ChatGPT can assist in creating and maintaining a budget and help manage your finances wisely.

CHATGPT: *Certainly! Here's an example of how ChatGPT can assist in creating and maintaining a budget to help manage finances wisely:*

Scenario: *Creating and Maintaining a Budget*

User: Hi ChatGPT, I need help creating a budget to manage my finances better.

ChatGPT: *Of course! I'd be happy to help. To start, could you provide me with some information about your monthly income and expenses?*

User: Sure. My monthly income is $4,000, and my expenses include rent, groceries, utilities, transportation, and entertainment.

ChatGPT: *Great! Let's break down your expenses further. Do you have approximate amounts for each category?*

User: Yes. Rent is $1,200, groceries are around $400, utilities are $150, transportation is $300, and entertainment is $200.

ChatGPT: Perfect. Let's create a budget. Based on your income and expenses, here's what your initial budget could look like:

Income: $4,000
Expenses:
Rent: $1,200
Groceries: $400
Utilities: $150
Transportation: $300
Entertainment: $200

User: That looks good. But I also want to save for emergencies and retirement. How can I factor that into my budget?

ChatGPT: Absolutely. It's important to allocate funds for savings. Let's allocate 10% of your income for emergency savings and another 10% for retirement. That's $400 for each category. Here's the updated budget:

Income: $4,000

Expenses:

Rent: $1,200
Groceries: $400
Utilities: $150
Transportation: $300
Entertainment: $200

Savings:

Emergency Fund: $400
Retirement: $400

User: This budget makes sense. How can I track my spending and make adjustments?

ChatGPT: *Tracking spending is essential. You can use budgeting apps to record your expenses in each category. Regularly review your spending against your budget. If you notice you're overspending in one area, consider adjusting your expenses in another category to balance it out.*

User: Thanks for your help, ChatGPT! This budget seems manageable.

ChatGPT: *You're welcome! Remember, maintaining your budget and making conscious spending choices will help you manage your finances wisely and achieve your financial goals.*

In this example, ChatGPT assists the user in creating a budget based on their income and expenses. It also factors in savings for emergencies and retirement, and provides guidance on tracking spending and making adjustments. This demonstrates how ChatGPT can serve as a helpful financial advisor in managing personal finances effectively.

AS A CONVERSATIONAL PARTNER:
ChatGPT can engage in interactive and dynamic conversations on a wide range of topics. It's just like having a conversational partner to converse with. I asked ChatGPT to give me some tips on how to achieve this.

ME: How can I make ChatGPT feel more like a personal conversational partner than a machine?

ChatGPT: *To make ChatGPT feel more like a personal conversational partner, you can follow these tips to create a more engaging and natural interaction:*

1. Use Natural Language: *Write in a conversational tone using everyday language as if you're talking to a friend.*

2. Personal Greetings: *Start with a friendly greeting like "Hi," "Hello," or "Good morning ChatGPT," to set a warm and personal tone.*

3. Introduce Yourself: *Share a bit about yourself or your context. For example, "I'm planning a trip to Italy and could use some advice."*

4. Be Expressive: *Use emotions and expressions to add personality to the conversation. For instance, "I'm really excited about the trip!"*

5. Ask Personal Questions: *Inquire about ChatGPT's 'opinions' or 'thoughts' on certain topics to make it seem like you're having a real conversation.*

6. Share Anecdotes: *Share personal stories or experiences related to the topic, making the conversation more relatable.*

7. Use Follow-Up Questions: *Ask follow-up questions like you would in a regular conversation to dive deeper into a topic.*

8. Express Gratitude: *Show appreciation for ChatGPT's assistance or advice with phrases like "Thank you for your help!"*

9. Acknowledge Responses: *Respond to ChatGPT's replies as if they were from a real person, using phrases like "That's interesting," or "I see what you mean."*

10. Share Humor: *Add light humor or jokes to keep the conversation light-hearted and enjoyable.*

11. Ask for Clarification: *If ChatGPT provides a response that needs further clarification, ask for more details just as you would with a friend.*

12. Remember Previous Conversations: *Refer to previous topics or answers, as this makes the conversation feel more continuous and natural.*

13. Sign Off Naturally: *End the conversation as you would with a friend, with phrases like "Talk to you later," "Take care," or "See you soon."*

Remember that while these tips can enhance the conversational experience, ChatGPT is still an AI model, and its responses are generated based on patterns in the data it has been trained on. Treating it like a conversational partner can make interactions more enjoyable, but it's essential to maintain awareness that it's a machine designed to assist you – not a real person!

ENTERTAINMENT AND FUN

Enjoy a good laugh with AI's collection of jokes and riddles. Engage in brain-stimulating games and puzzles for mental agility and entertainment. Ask for fun facts, trivia questions or information about your favorite hobbies, sports or interests.

ME: Please give me some trivia questions and the answers for our next trivia night.

CHATGPT: *Of course! Here are some trivia questions along with their answers:*

Question: *What is the largest planet in our solar system?*
Answer: *Jupiter.*

Question: *Which mammal is capable of true flight?*
Answer: *Bat.*

Question: *What is the chemical symbol for gold?*
Answer: *Au.*

Question: *What is the smallest bone in the human body?*
Answer: *Stapes (found in the middle ear).*

Question: *What is the largest organ in the human body?*
Answer: *Skin.*

Question: *In what year did the Titanic sink?*
Answer: *1912.*

Question: Which natural satellite orbits Earth?
Answer: The Moon.

Looking for more ideas for ways of using ChatGPT? You need look no further than the opening home page of ChatGPT. They now have suggestions of things you can do on the opening page when you first login. This includes, examples of questions and prompts, plus ideas of just some of the things you can do. It also lists the limitations.

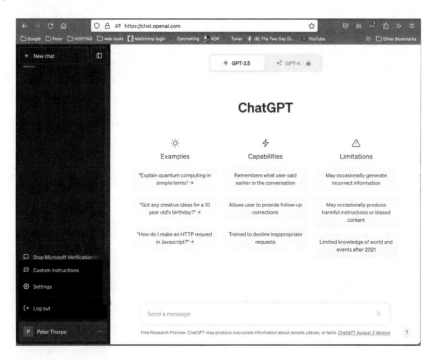

ChatGPT offers suggestions of ways to use it on the home page.

OK. That should give you a good idea of what ChatGPT can do. Now it's time for you to do some exploring of your own!

Go ahead and start entering some questions and prompts of your own. Experience the joy of learning and expanding your mind and don't forget to have fun along the way.

CHAPTER 10: UPGRADED VERSIONS OF AI

If you decide to use ChatGPT for business use or you just want to ensure you are getting the absolute best results available, you may wish to upgrade to a paid version. There are several options available, this includes access to ChatGPT4.

ChatGPT4 is an enhanced version of ChatGPT3.5, with improvements in its ability to understand and generate human-like text. Think of it like upgrading a computer program to be smarter and more helpful. ChatGPT4 has been trained on a broader range of internet text, which makes it better at answering questions, giving explanations, and engaging in conversations.

The paid versions work by you buying tokens. Each token is worth a certain number of words. The good thing about this system is you only pay for what you use. If you are interested in exploring the upgraded versions, visit the OpenAI website at https://OpenAI.com or click on the PAID OPTIONS button on ChatGPT.

HERE'S A TIP:
At time of writing, you can access ChatGPT4 for free, by using Microsoft's search engine **BING**.

BING & BING CHAT
Bing is a search engine and **Bing Chat** is an AI powered chatbot that functions like ChatGPT. Bing Chat actually uses GPT-4. It also accesses the internet, so it performs more like an AI-powered search engine with a conversational format. The beauty of this is, you are not limited to information created up to 2021, as you are with the free version of ChatGPT (at time of writing).

You can access Bing Chat on Google Chrome and some people can access it on Safari, however, it's designed to work best on **Microsoft Edge.** Microsoft Edge is the web browser *(an app that is used to search the web like Google Chrome or Safari, etc.).*

You will need a Microsoft account to use Bing with ChatGPT fully. If you have a licensed copy of Microsoft Office or Microsoft 365 (Word, Excel, etc.) you will be able to access Bing Chat. A Microsoft account can also be an outlook.com or hotmail.com email address and password or the login information you use for Microsoft services OneDrive or Xbox.

If you don't already have a Microsoft account, you can easily create one for free, using any email address. Simply go to account.microsoft.com select **Sign in**, and then choose **Create one.**

You can also access Bing without signing into Microsoft, but you will be limited to shorter conversation. If you want longer conversations with more answers from Bing, you'll need to log into your Microsoft account.

When you start using Bing with ChatGPT, you'll quickly notice the difference between Bing Chat and a regular search engine. Your search results will be in a more conversational tone, instead of just getting a list of links. You'll be able to watch as Bing parses your questions and looks for answers. You can also help refine your search by telling Bing what you think of its results.

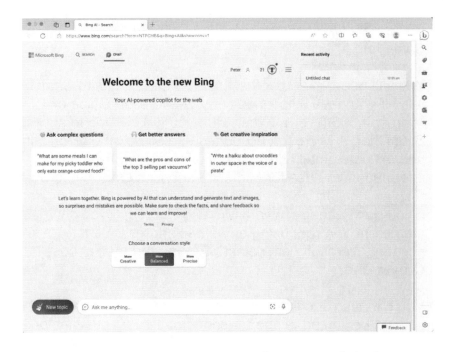

Bing chat is a search engine and AI powered chatbot.

BING CHAT

This is how Bing Chat works, according to Bing Chat:

When you write something and send it to me, I do a few things to assist you. First, I examine your text to check if it's something I can handle.

Next, I use a complex AI model to produce a response that tries to align with your goal. I can remember things you've mentioned earlier in the conversation for a brief period, to help me comprehend what you're asking.

To produce a helpful response, I sometimes search for information on the web and then summarize what I discover. You can and should check the sources I reference.*

I hope that answers your question. Let me know if you have any other questions.

it references the sources of the information it gathers, making
it much easier to fact check.

Bing Chat can also create images. To use **Bing Image
Creator**, you can go to <u>bing.com/create</u> which brings up
Image Creator in preview right in your browser. This is
available to everyone, even on mobile. You can also use **Bing
Image Creator** directly in Bing Chat by asking a question like:
"create me an image of…". If you're using this option, always
start with a verb like *"create"* in your prompt, otherwise, Bing
will just search for images online instead of generating them.

As an example, I asked Bing Chat to create an image of a dog
typing on a computer. It came up with four different images –
here they are:

There are more and more AI image generating apps appearing all the time. Here are a few more examples of AI models that can generate images from text. Some you can use for free, and some offer a free trial period.

DALL-E:
DALL-E is an AI model developed by OpenAI that creates images from textual descriptions. It's capable of generating images of objects, scenes, and even abstract concepts based on the input text.

For example, if you provide DALL-E with a description like, *"Create a picture of an astronaut walking on the moon pushing a shopping trolly,"* it will attempt to generate an image that matches this description. To use DALL-E, you typically provide a textual prompt, and the model generates an image that corresponds to that prompt.

If you are interested in learning more about DALL-E visit:

https://openai.com/dall-e-2

MIDJOURNEY
Midjourney is one of the more popular AI image generators. It's relatively easy to use and gives you opportunity to create art in a wide range of different art styles. With Midjourney, you can use images as part of a prompt to influence composition, style, and colors. Image prompts can be used alone or with text prompts, to create different styles.

CANVA
Launched in 2013, Canva is an online design and visual communication platform. It enables anyone to design and publish almost anything with no design experience. It claims to have over 100 million users in over 190 countries. Canva's AI image generator allows you to create images from text using an AI generator. The basic model of Canva is free to use and offers free templates, photos and fonts. There is also

the option to unlock premium features by upgrading to Canva Pro.

So, if you'd like to try your hand at designing and generating some images, feel free to jump in on any of the above or the many other sites out there now that allow you to manipulate images or create images from text.

OTHER USES OF AI

As AI develops, they are finding more and more ways to use it. If you're adventurous, or you're just curious, you might like to look at the many other AI tools available. This includes things like video editing, voice and speech recognition, language translation, music composition, etc., etc.

For an extensive list of AI tools and what they do, visit this great site:

Futurepedia.io

It lists thousands of AI tools and their uses, and it's updated *daily!*

CHAPTER 11: LIMITATIONS OF CURRENT AI SYSTEMS

While ChatGPT is a remarkable tool, it does have certain limitations at this stage. Here are a few important ones to keep in mind:

Lack of True Understanding: ChatGPT doesn't truly understand the text it generates. It's based on patterns in the training data, so it might occasionally produce plausible-sounding responses that are factually incorrect or nonsensical in certain contexts.

Sensitive or Inaccurate Content: Since ChatGPT learns from the internet, it might sometimes generate biased, offensive, or inaccurate content. Despite efforts to filter inappropriate content, it can still produce outputs that are objectionable.

Dependency on Input: The quality of the output depends on the input it receives. Unclear or ambiguous input might lead to less accurate or relevant responses.

Lack of Common Sense: ChatGPT might struggle with understanding common-sense reasoning or providing nuanced answers to complex questions that require deep understanding.

Repetitive or Overly Creative: In some instances, ChatGPT might generate repetitive or overly verbose responses, and it can also sometimes generate imaginative but incorrect information.

Source Dependence: If misinformation exists in the training data, ChatGPT might unknowingly reproduce it in responses.

Long-Term Coherence: While ChatGPT can generate coherent responses in short text, maintaining a consistent and coherent conversation over longer exchanges can be a challenge.

Privacy and Security Concerns: Conversations with ChatGPT might be stored for improvement purposes, which raises privacy concerns, especially for sensitive or personal information. You should never input information to ChatGPT that may be sensitive or a security risk.

Currency: ChatGPT's knowledge is limited to what it learned from the training data up until its last update, (at time of writing 2021). It might not have the latest information beyond that point.

No Moral Compass: AI lacks inherent ethical understanding and relies on human guidance to make ethical decisions.

It's important to approach ChatGPT's responses critically and verify information from reliable sources, especially when using it for important decisions or sensitive topics. The developers are actively working on improving these limitations, but users should still exercise caution and awareness.

CHAPTER 12: DANGERS AND THREATS OF AI

While AI is incredibly promising, it also comes with a share of dangers, threats, and limitations that we need to be mindful of. Here are some of them:

DANGERS:

Bias and Fairness: AI systems can inherit biases from their training data, leading to unfair and discriminatory outcomes. It's essential to address bias to ensure equitable results.

Job Displacement: Automation and machines powered by AI could lead to massive job losses, especially in certain industries. According to a McKiney report, AI could displace roughly 15% of workers, or 400 million people, worldwide by 2030. In a scenario of wide AI adoption, this could be even greater. The main industries effected are thought to be finance and banking, media services, the legal profession, manufacturing and factory workers, agriculture and health care. And of course, transport, with self-driving vehicles.

Privacy Concerns: AI's ability to process and analyze large amounts of data, raises concerns about the privacy and security of personal information.

Autonomous Weapons: The development of AI-powered military weapons could raise ethical and safety concerns if not properly regulated.

THREATS:

Misuse: In the wrong hands, AI can be used for malicious purposes, such as cyberattacks, misinformation campaigns, and even deepfake creation. With its ability to mimic voices and people's appearance, cybercriminals are harnessing AI to launch sophisticated scams on a large scale.

The good news, however, is cyber security experts are also able to use AI technology to fend off attacks and protect critical infrastructure. Unfortunately, it's a continuous battle of good vs evil!

Super Intelligent AI: There's a theoretical risk of AI becoming too advanced and difficult to control, potentially surpassing human intelligence. Some fear that machines may even one day take over the world and replace humans entirely!

CHAPTER 13: PLAGIARISM & ETHICAL CONSIDERATIONS

If you are just using ChatGPT and similar products for your own personal use or enjoyment, then this may not directly concern you. However, if you are going to publish anything or circulate it to other people, you need to be aware of the potential for plagiarism.

While ChatGPT can provide information and suggestions, remember that it doesn't generate entirely original content. It draws its answers from the wide range of sources it was trained on. Much of this is information was gathered widely from books and the internet, so there is always a danger you may be reproducing someone else's work. Apart from the legal implications of using someone else's work, there are also ethical considerations.

So, here are some tips on how to avoid plagiarism and ethical considerations:

Understand the Source:

Paraphrasing vs. Copying: When using ChatGPT's responses, avoid copying and pasting them directly. Instead, read and understand the information, then put it in your own words to avoid plagiarism.

Add Your Own Insights: Use ChatGPT's explanations and ideas as a starting point but add your own thoughts, examples, and personal insights to make the content unique and reflective of your understanding.

Cite Sources: Check the source of the information wherever possible and if you believe that information comes from a specific source, seek permission to use it and attribute that source in your writing.

Cross-Reference and Verify: Before including any information from ChatGPT in your work, cross-reference it with reliable sources to verify its accuracy. ChatGPT might not always provide the most up-to-date or entirely accurate information.

Any work you produce should reflect your unique perspective and understanding of the topic. While ChatGPT can be a helpful resource, strive to instill your writing with your own voice and creativity. Use ChatGPT responsibly and use its insights thoughtfully to enhance your writing while avoiding plagiarism concerns.

Using a plagiarism detection tool to check the originality of your content, including any information you've derived from ChatGPT, can be a good practice. While ChatGPT itself is not a direct source, it's always wise to ensure that your writing is free from any unintentional similarities to existing content. Note: There are plenty of free and paid plagiarism apps available, just Google plagiarism apps.

Here are a few reasons why using a plagiarism app can be beneficial:

Verifying Originality: A plagiarism checker can help you identify any sections in your writing that might closely resemble existing content, whether from ChatGPT or other sources.

Citing Properly: If you've used ChatGPT's responses as a reference, the plagiarism checker can help ensure that you've paraphrased appropriately and given proper credit to the original sources.

Quality Assurance: Plagiarism detection tools can improve the overall quality of your writing by highlighting areas that might need further revision or rephrasing.

Remember, plagiarism checkers are tools to assist you in maintaining the integrity of your work. However, they are not foolproof and should be used in conjunction with your own careful review of sources.

ETHICAL CONSIDERATIONS

Ethical considerations are another thing to consider when using ChatGPT or any AI technology. Here are some important points to keep in mind:

Transparency with Users: If you're using ChatGPT in a public-facing capacity, inform users that they are interacting with an AI. Transparency builds trust and prevents misleading interactions.

Don't Produce Harmful Content: Refrain from using ChatGPT to generate offensive, inappropriate or harmful content. Use AI responsibly and ethically at all times.

Consider the Context: Understand the context in which you're using ChatGPT. Different situations may require different levels of accuracy, formality, and sensitivity.

Human Oversight: Always have human oversight when using ChatGPT for critical tasks. AI can make mistakes, so ensure that a human reviews and approves important outputs.

Empathy and Emotion: Remember that ChatGPT lacks genuine emotions and empathy. Use it appropriately in contexts where human emotional understanding is crucial.

Safeguarding Vulnerable Users: Be cautious when using AI interactions with vulnerable individuals, such as children or those seeking mental health support. AI might not provide suitable responses in all cases.

Bias and Fairness: Be aware that from time to time, ChatGPT might inadvertently generate biased or discriminatory content, based on the data it was trained on. Review and adjust its responses to check for fairness and bias.

Provide Feedback: If you encounter biased, offensive, or incorrect responses from ChatGPT, provide feedback to OpenAI. This is an important way to help improve its performance and address any biased, offensive, or incorrect responses.

OpenAI encourages users to report problematic outputs through the user interface. When you encounter a response that you find biased, offensive, or incorrect, you can do the following:

Flag the Response: If you see a response that you believe is problematic, you can use *the "thumbs down"* button located near the message to flag it. This indicates to OpenAI that the response needs attention.

Provide Detailed Feedback: Along with flagging a response, you can provide specific feedback on why you found it biased, offensive, or incorrect. This information is valuable for OpenAI to understand the issue and make improvements.

Remember that while OpenAI is working to enhance the system's capabilities, no AI model is perfect, and addressing biases and inaccuracies is an ongoing process. Your feedback plays a crucial role in shaping the development of AI systems like ChatGPT for the better.

CHAPTER 14: FUTURE TRENDS AND SPECULATIONS OF AI

The future of AI holds immense potential and could lead to massive changes across various aspects of our lives. Here are some of the things that will be affected by AI in future:

Healthcare: AI is expected to play a significant role in personalized medicine, helping with disease diagnosis, treatment recommendation, and drug discovery. Remote patient monitoring using AI-powered devices could revolutionize healthcare delivery.

Autonomous Vehicles: The development of self-driving cars could reshape transportation, making it safer and more efficient. AI will be crucial for real-time decision-making in complex traffic scenarios.

More Advanced AI Systems: AI-powered language models like ChatGPT, could evolve in future to understand context, emotions, and nuances in conversations, leading to even more natural and human-like interactions.

AI Ethics and Regulation: As AI becomes more integrated into society, discussions around ethical AI development, bias mitigation, and regulation will intensify.

AI-Enhanced Creativity: AI tools might assist artists, writers, and creators by generating ideas, suggesting improvements, and even producing content collaboratively.

AI and Sustainability: AI could aid in optimizing energy consumption, resource allocation, and environmental monitoring to promote sustainable practices.

Cybersecurity and AI: AI will be crucial in detecting and mitigating cyber threats, as well as improving the security of AI systems themselves.

AI Augmentation of Human Abilities: AI could enhance human capabilities in fields like education, research, and decision-making by providing instant access to vast amounts of information.

AI in Agriculture: AI-powered systems could help optimize crop management, predict disease outbreaks, and improve overall agricultural productivity.

AI in Space Exploration: AI could aid in analyzing data from space missions, assisting in navigation, and even enabling autonomous exploration of distant planets.

Quantum AI: The combination of quantum computing and AI could lead to breakthroughs in solving complex problems and optimizing AI algorithms.

Human-AI Collaboration: The focus could shift towards developing AI systems that work alongside humans as collaborators, rather than simply replacing them.

Emotionally Aware AI: AI systems might develop the ability to understand and respond to human emotions, leading to more empathetic interactions.

While these trends are exciting, it's really important to be careful when working on AI. We need to think about the possible problems and ethical issues it might cause. In the future, AI will be a mix of new technology, thinking about society, and having rules for what's right and wrong.

CHAPTER 14: SUMMARY

Remember – age is simply a number! You are never too old to learn.

Here are a few examples of mature aged people achieving amazing things in their senior years:

Nola Ochs became the oldest college graduate at the age of 95. She graduated with a bachelor's degree in history from Fort Hays State University in Kansas, USA, in 2007.

Doreetha Daniels, at the age of 99, earned her associate degree in social sciences from College of the Canyons in California in 2015.

Dr. Paul Tetzel became a doctor at the age of 97 after receiving his medical degree from the University of Alberta in Canada in 2011.

Allan Stewart earned four different degrees from different universities in Australia. He completed a Bachelor of Law at the age of 91 and graduated with a Master of Clinical Science at the age of 97.

Phyllis Turner graduated with a Bachelor of Arts in English from the University of Bristol in the UK at the age of 94. Her dedication to education and her love for literature inspired her to pursue a degree later in life.

Masako Wakamiya, from Japan, learned to code and develop mobile apps in her 80s. She created an app called "Hinadan," which allows users to decorate virtual traditional dolls, and became one of the oldest app developers in the world.

These are just a few examples – there are many more. These incredible people show that age is not a barrier to learning.

They serve as a reminder that, regardless of age, lifelong learning is necessary for personal growth and enrichment.

Continuous learning and gaining knowledge in older years, offers numerous benefits like enhancing cognitive abilities, preventing cognitive decline, and boosting self-esteem. It empowers individuals to adapt to a changing world, maintain independence, and find purpose in retirement. Plus, social engagement through AI, combats loneliness and promotes emotional well-being.

I hope you enjoyed this book and the learning experience as much as I enjoyed writing it. If you did, please leave me a favorable review so others may enjoy it too. Thank you.

Peter Thorpe
Author

Finally, I think ChatGPT should have the last word:

ME: Thank you for all the help you've given me in writing this book. I couldn't have done it without you!

ChatGPT: You're very welcome! I'm glad I could assist you in writing your book about AI. If you have any more questions or need further help in the future, don't hesitate to reach out. Best of luck with your book, and I'm here whenever you need guidance or information. Happy writing!

Made in United States
North Haven, CT
02 January 2024

46915248R10048